NEIL PATRICK HARRIS

HARRIS

AND

DAVID BURTKA

POWER COUPLES™

NEIL PATRICK HARRIS

AND

DAVID BURTKA

Jason Porterfield

Rosen
YA™
New York

Published in 2020 by The Rosen Publishing Group, Inc.
29 East 21st Street, New York, NY 10010

Library of Congress Cataloging-in-Publication Data

Names: Porterfield, Jason, author.
Title: Neil Patrick Harris and David Burtka / Jason Porterfield.
Description: First edition. | New York: Rosen Publishing, 2020. | Series: Power couples | Audience: Grades 7–12. | Includes bibliographical references and index.
Identifiers: LCCN 2018051633| ISBN 9781508188940 (library bound) | ISBN 9781508188933 (paperback) Subjects: LCSH: Harris, Neil Patrick, 1973– —Juvenile literature. | Burtka, David—Juvenile literature. | Gay actors—United States—Biography—Juvenile literature. | Gay couples—United States—Biography—Juvenile literature. Classification: LCC PN2286.5 .P67 2020 | DDC 791.4502/80922 [B]—dc23 LC record available at https://lccn.loc.gov/2018051633

Manufactured in China

On the cover: On February 8, 2015, David Burtka and Neil Patrick Harris arrive at the Fifty-Seventh Annual Grammy Awards, held at the Staples Center in Los Angeles, California.

CONTENTS

INTRODUCTION

In 2018, the season two finale of the hit streaming show *A Series of Unfortunate Events* was made available to audiences. As the episode unfolded, the evil Count Olaf menaced the audience of a carnival while trying to cheat the Baudelaire siblings out of

Neil Patrick Harris (*left*) and David Burtka attend a Ringling Bros. and Barnum & Bailey Circus show with their children, Harper and Gideon, in 2013.

their fortune. The children had to rely on their wits to defeat Count Olaf and escape from danger.

Regular viewers of the show likely knew that Count Olaf was played by actor Neil Patrick Harris. They might not have realized that the three audience members who had speaking parts in the episode were Harris's husband, David Burtka, and their young children, twins Harper and Gideon. Their characters, Mr. Willums and his children Skip and Trixie, ask Count Olaf questions about the gruesome carnival performance they were about to see.

For the Burtka-Harris family, appearing together in the show was another milestone in their adventurous life together. Harris and Burtka both experienced phenomenal success as actors. Harris has taken on challenging roles since first becoming famous in the late 1980s as the star of the hit television show *Doogie Howser, M.D.* Burtka was a well-regarded actor in stage dramas and musicals who went on to become a professional chef. Both have put their many talents on display in theatrical productions, television shows, and movies. They've both seen their careers take startling new directions. Burtka has helped judge cooking shows. Harris has hosted major awards events.

The family has become a social media sensation. Harris regularly posts photos and provides updates on social networking sites such as Twitter. Together as a couple since 2004, Burtka and Harris are comfortable sharing the spotlight as one of Hollywood's power couples, with their combined influence helping to set trends and standards at levels far higher than they could accomplish separately. Their sense of style, the look of their home, and even the meals they prepare together have been on display to the world.

In addition to being trendsetters and entertainers, both men have been active in trying to make the world a better place for their twins, who were born in 2010. They have worked hard to promote rights for lesbian, gay, bisexual, transsexual, and queer (LGBTQ) individuals. They have supported other worthy causes, such as reducing hunger and promoting new ways to deliver medical supplies to people living in impoverished areas. Together, the Burtka-Harris family can look forward to creating more entertaining moments, and working to make an impact on the world around them.

CHAPTER 1

A STAR-STUDDED CHILDHOOD

Neil Patrick Harris was born on June 15, 1973, in Albuquerque, New Mexico. He was the second child of Sheila Gail Scott and Ronald Gene Harris. His brother, Brian, was three years older.

The Harrises were a successful couple living in a very small town called Ruidoso, New Mexico. Both worked in Albuquerque as attorneys.

Sheila Harris and Ron Harris stand with their son Neil during a charity event in 1989, when Neil was first becoming a star.

NEW MEXICO LIFE

Ruidoso was very rural, and life there was quiet. Neil's parents often worked long hours in the city, seeing clients and pursuing cases. He and Brian were given considerable freedom to play and experience the great outdoors around their home.

Brian and his friends often let Neil tag along in their activities. According to an article in *Rolling Stone*, Brian and his friends thought Neil was funny and enjoyed his company. The brothers and

Ruidoso is a small town in rural New Mexico. As children, Neil, his brother, and their friends spent a lot of time playing in the surrounding woods.

their friends spent much time fishing, exploring the nearby woods, and riding their bikes around Ruidoso. They came to know the countryside well, memorizing the trees and paths they encountered. At home, he and Brian listened to their father play the guitar or sing, or they listened to records. The Harris family had a large collection of Broadway recordings that the boys often played.

> " I love seeking out how things work. I wanted to know those secrets and discover those mysteries, and the library made that search possible in a small town in New Mexico."
> —NEIL PATRICK HARRIS

When he wasn't roaming around in the woods, Neil enjoyed reading and learning magic tricks. In his autobiography, *Neil Patrick Harris: Choose Your Own Autobiography*, he wrote about being a young child when he discovered that he liked to entertain people and make them laugh. His first job was in a bookstore when he was ten or eleven years old. He helped do the store's inventory, created store displays, and worked the cash register. The job helped fuel his love of reading. He sometimes read as many as forty or fifty books per month when he was in elementary school. As reported by Haisten Willis of the *Atlanta Journal-Constitution*, Harris told a gathering of the American Library Association: "I love seeking out how things work. I wanted to know those secrets and discover those mysteries, and the library made that search possible in a small town in New Mexico."

THE ART OF MAGIC

Everybody knows Neil Patrick Harris as an actor, a singer, a dancer, an awards show host, and a writer, but the versatile showman is also an accomplished magician who performs real magic tricks. Like many kids, Harris was fascinated by magic from a young age. He saved up his allowance to buy magic tricks from a magic shop during family visits to Albuquerque. His enthusiasm never faded, and Harris continues to dazzle spectators with magic tricks during interviews, award shows, and public appearances. He bent a spoon using his mind for Ellen DeGeneres, predicted the Oscar winners while hosting the Academy Awards, and correctly guessed which word an audience member picked from his book for kids, *The Magical Misfits*. Harris also served as president of the Academy of Magical Arts, an organization that promotes the practice of magic.

In 1983, Brian and some of his friends tried out for roles in a production of *The Wizard of Oz* that was being staged at a local high school. As usual, Neil tagged along to join in the fun. Brian auditioned for a role as one of the Munchkins living in Oz. Neil landed the part of Toto, Dorothy's little dog that makes the journey to Oz with her.

Neil loved being on stage, according to his autobiography. He tried out for more local theater parts, often getting cast in productions that needed a child to play certain roles. These parts nurtured his fast-developing love for acting. He kept acting when the family moved to Albuquerque in 1988. Neil's family members encouraged his interest in the theater, but they wanted him to be realistic about his passion. His parents felt that becoming an actor and making a living at it was an impossible goal for Neil, according to the *Rolling Stone* article.

HOLLYWOOD COMES CALLING

Sheila and Ronald Harris decided to try to make Neil realize acting was not something he could do professionally. When he was twelve or thirteen, they allowed him to attend a drama camp held at New Mexico State University in Las Cruces, according to *Rolling Stone*. Neil would see how many young adults shared his talent and passion for acting and realize that there was too much competition for him to become a professional actor.

The idea of discouraging Neil's acting ambitions by showing him stiff competition backfired spectacularly. One of the people running the camp was Tony Award-winning playwright Mark Medoff. According to a story by KVIA News 7, Medoff thought that Neil had the kind of acting talent that could turn him into a star.

Neil had no idea that the theater camp was supposed to discourage him. He had a wonderful time and formed a connection with Medoff. He returned home feeling that acting was something he wanted to do with his life, he later wrote.

Medoff was also a screenwriter who wrote movies, with some success. Shortly before the camp started, he sold a script for a movie called *Clara's Heart* (1988). He thought Neil would be a perfect fit in the film and had him put together an audition tape. Neil was cast as a spoiled boy named David who was central to the movie's plot. Neil would be acting in a Hollywood movie. It was a

Whoopi Goldberg and Neil Patrick Harris share a scene in the film *Clara's Heart*. He and Goldberg became good friends on the set.

dizzying change for a thirteen-year-old boy whose parents were still not sure that acting was the right course for him.

Neil's role was as the son of one of the adult characters. He worked closely alongside the movie's star, actress Whoopi Goldberg. Goldberg played the title role as a maid who looked after David. Goldberg, director Bob Mulligan, and the rest of the cast and crew patiently showed Neil how to act in front of a camera.

Much of the rest of Neil's life was unchanged. He was with his family during filming. He was still expected to study. When filming was completed, he and his family went back to Albuquerque and continued to live their lives in much the same way as before.

SUDDEN STARDOM

Clara's Heart performed poorly when it was released into theaters, although it received mainly positive reviews. Some reviews singled out Neil. Neil was nominated for a Golden Globe Award for his work as David.

More film roles followed as people in Hollywood learned about Neil's talent. Soon after *Clara's Heart,* he was quickly cast in a children's fantasy film called *Purple People Eater* (1988) and the made-for-TV movie *Too Good to Be True* (1988). Those projects did not garner any awards nominations or special notice for Neil, but both were positive experiences. Like his time on the set of *Clara's Heart*, Neil was able to work with generous Hollywood stars and learn more about acting from them.

At first, life changed very little for the Harris family. Neil's parents still worked, although they would take time off when he was working on a film. He would return to Albuquerque between projects, where he had begun attending La Cueva High School. When he was working, he received tutoring on sets so he could keep up with his studies. Neil did very well in his classes despite the occasional time away from school. He lived as normal a life as possible, following his passion for learning new magic tricks. He and his friends in Albuquerque often got together to make funny home videos that parodied real movies. Neil, as revealed in his autobiography, was having a great time as a young actor.

THE BREAKOUT ROLE

Neil enjoyed working on films and loved acting, as he later wrote in his autobiography. His parents had become comfortable with the fact that he was talented enough to hold his own alongside established actors. He worked on more television projects, including a made-for-TV movie *Cold Sassy Tree* (1989) that was adapted from a novel of the same name by Olive Anne Burns. The movie was about a woman from the North who caused a scandal

In *Cold Sassy Tree*, Neil plays a character from the early 1900s named Will Tweedy. Here he drives an antique automobile with stars Faye Dunaway and Richard Widmark.

by marrying a Southern store owner shortly after his wife died. The movie starred film legend Faye Dunaway as the female lead, with Neil playing a supporting role and serving as the story's narrator.

He worked on another made-for-TV movie called *Home Fires Burning* (1989) about a soldier returning to his hometown after the end of World War II to find that changes had taken place while he was away. Neil played one of the soldier's sons.

Neil also had his first part in a television series, taking a role in an episode of the short-lived drama *B.L. Stryker*. The show starred Burt Reynolds as the title character, a private detective who lived on a boat in Florida. Neil played a boy who had unusual religious ideas and whose parents had hired the detective to help him.

In 1989, at age fifteen, he had another chance to audition for a role on a television series about a teenager who worked in a hospital. Neil was competing against hundreds of other talented young actors for a role in the pilot episode of a series that would become *Doogie Howser, M.D.* The pilot episode would be shown to audiences to help television studio executives decide whether they wanted to invest in taking a full season of the show.

Producer Steven Bochco liked what he saw in Neil's audition and wanted him to play the main character, according to Harris's autobiography. However, some of the other people involved in the casting process didn't think Neil had the right set of skills to be successful in the role, as described in his autobiography. Bochco eventually won the argument. Two days before taping was scheduled to begin, Neil and his parents learned that he had been cast in the pilot as Doogie Howser. The series introduced him to families across the country.

CHAPTER 2

HANDLING THE SPOTLIGHT

Accepting the role of Doogie Howser was not a decision Neil and his family took lightly. As Harris related in his autobiography, before he accepted the role, show producer Steven Bochco sat down with the family and explained that their lives would change drastically. If the show was a success, the taping schedule would be far more intense than anything Neil had experienced before. His other television work and his movie roles had given him the space to return to Albuquerque and experience life as a normal teenager. Television shows, on the other

As a teenager working in a hospital, the character Doogie Howser often had to deal with adults who were skeptical of his abilities because of his age. Neil appears here in the role during the TV program's first season.

hand, were long-term projects. He would have to be prepared to spend long days on the set while also balancing his school work.

Neil would have to move to California to work on the show. Because he was still a minor, at least one of his parents would also have to move with him. The Harris family took Bochco's offer of the role and his advice seriously. Both of Neil's parents decided to put their careers as lawyers on hold, according to a *People* magazine profile by Joanne Kaufman. They would both move to Los Angeles with Neil.

A TELEVISION SUCCESS

Doogie Howser, M.D. was picked up to run on the ABC television network during prime time beginning in the fall of 1989. The network initially opposed Neil's casting as the show's lead, but allowed him to continue in the role after the pilot episode was well received by audiences. Bochco's instincts, as described in Harris's autobiography, that Neil would be perfect in the role, were correct.

The show featured Neil as a brilliant teenager named Doogie Howser who balanced a medical career with the everyday pressures of teenage life. The character was written as someone so brilliant that he had perfect SAT scores and graduated from medical school at age fourteen. He turned sixteen in the show's first episode and still lived at home.

The character was also motivated to become a doctor after undergoing treatment for leukemia as a child. As a second-year medical resident, Doogie Howser was determined to give patients the best care possible. He also wanted to prove to the skeptical adults working in this hospital that he belonged there despite his young age.

Each episode of the show addressed some serious topic, such as racism, the AIDS epidemic, homophobia, and aging. Doogie struggles to be accepted by his adult colleagues and by his teen peers. His unique situation leads to sequences such as his friends sneaking into his home through his bedroom window and his writing prescriptions to patients despite being too young to legally drink alcohol. The character also experiences events that are typical in the lives of many teens. He breaks up with his girlfriend and eventually moves in to his own apartment. As time passes, Doogie even becomes disillusioned with his medical career and questions his reasons for wanting to become a doctor.

DOOGIE'S DIARY

It's not unusual for a young person to keep a diary. Doogie Howser, however, was precocious even in his journal entries. In 1979, Doogie's father agreed to buy him a computer only if he'd write a journal entry every night. Back then, few families owned personal computers. In the show, Doogie writes on April 27, 1993, that it was his entry number 4,773.

Doogie Howser, M.D. wrapped up every episode with Doogie's daily entry, each a few sentences long. Like most kids, Doogie wrote about his feelings, observations, and important events in his life. The entries often provide insight into his character. In his very first entry, sixteen-year-old Doogie writes about getting his driver's license and losing a patient. Throughout the series, his writing provides wry commentary on everything from relationships to confronting prejudice to asserting his independence.

Some television critics were skeptical of the series at first. The idea that a sixteen-year-old could become a doctor was too outrageous for some. The sometimes formulaic plots of individual episodes and the lessons Doogie learned in each were occasionally seen as heavy-handed. Audiences responded warmly to the show and to Neil in the role of Doogie. The series finished its first season in the spring of 1990 as the thirty-second most-watched show on prime time television, as reported in an article in the *Chicago Tribune*.

The show's producers felt that Neil was a major part of that success, according to the *Chicago Tribune* story. Audiences saw him as charming, intelligent, and naive as Doogie navigated through each episode. He was able to give the character a level of internal conflict while also being relatable for teenage viewers.

Neil's work on the show was recognized with several awards during its run, according to the Internet Movie Database. He won the Young Artist Award for Best Young Actor Starring in a Television Series three times, in 1991, 1992, and 1993. He was also nominated for a Golden Globe Award for Best Performance by an Actor in a TV-Series—

Members of the cast of *Doogie Howser, M.D.* pose together after stars Neil Patrick Harris (*fourth from right*) and Max Casella (*on the left next to Neil*) each receive Peoples' Choice Awards in 1990.

27

Comedy/Musical in 1992. Bochco's trust in Neil to give his show life was rewarded.

PUBLIC EYE, PRIVATE LIFE

Doogie Howser, M.D. was a popular hit and made Neil into a major star. Neil became a teen idol and was featured on magazine covers. Like the character he played, Neil also had to balance his professional life and his life as a teen. He had his parents with him in Los Angeles to help him manage some of the pressures he faced. Neil avoided the partying lifestyle that many teen stars fell into at that time. He also remained connected to New Mexico. He graduated from La Cueva High School in 1991 with highest honors. He later credited the tutors he worked with while he was on the set for his academic achievements.

He also faced a personal conflict within himself. Neil had known he was attracted to other boys since before his first film role, he wrote in his autobiography. Society was just beginning to be more accepting of LGBTQ individuals. Actors and actresses often hid their sexuality to avoid a backlash from the public. Neil had very few gay role models and no one to talk to about his sexuality. He dated several girls during his teen years, despite the fact that he was not attracted to them.

Neil focused on his work and school while keeping his sexuality a secret. Becoming a TV star meant that he had more responsibilities, including interacting

The success Neil Patrick Harris experienced as the star of *Doogie Howser, M.D.* didn't change him from the friendly and outgoing person he had been before becoming famous.

with fans. With help from his parents, he read and responded to fan mail and attended events where he met with people who loved *Doogie Howser, M.D.* He was interviewed for magazine articles, was photographed many times for teen magazines, and even made a guest appearance as Doogie Howser in an episode of the animated show *The Simpsons*. He didn't mind interacting with fans, he later noted in his autobiography. However, he disliked being seen as a teen heartthrob, according to Joanne Kaufman's *People* magazine profile of the young actor. His questions about his own sexuality made him very uncomfortable with being presented as a romantic ideal to teen girls, he later recounted.

DOOGIE'S END

Doogie Howser, M.D. was canceled by ABC in 1993 because of a drop in ratings. The audiences that had once tuned in every week to watch the young doctor struggle to find himself tuned in to other shows. By the time it concluded, the series had run for ninety-seven episodes over four seasons. It had been a major success for ABC and Bochco, while giving Harris's career a major boost.

Harris was nineteen when the series finale was aired. The last episode showed Doogie resigning from the hospital. Instead of practicing medicine, the character would travel to Europe and learn to be himself after so many years of focusing on his goal.

Doogie Howser, M.D. had made Harris famous and successful. He enjoyed working on the show, but it had a downside. He was so recognizable that many people who had never met him assumed he would be just like Doogie Howser. Harris wrote in his autobiography about how he wanted to avoid being turned down for other types of acting roles because he was associated with the Doogie character.

I got overwhelmed with Los Angeles. I was still figuring out who I was as a man, and that was a very bizarre magnifying glass, to be doing that. Especially having finished a job that I was recognized for."

—NEIL PATRICK HARRIS

Harris had also become very self-conscious while he was working on *Doogie Howser, M.D.* Like the character he played, he felt that he had spent so much time chasing his goal of becoming an actor that he didn't really know how to be himself, according to *Rolling Stone*.

He had earned a great deal of money while working on the show and had been careful to save most of his earnings. He could afford to take a short break from acting and figure out his next move. He returned to Albuquerque for a while, sharing a house out in the countryside with some friends and spending his days rock climbing. As he told the *AV Club*:

I got overwhelmed with Los Angeles. I was still figuring out who I was as a man, and that was a very bizarre magnifying glass, to be doing that. Especially having finished a job that I was recognized for.

Harris attended self-improvement seminars. Such sessions encouraged participants to ask themselves hard questions about their goals in life and helped them plan how to make those goals a reality. The seminars helped him recover some of his confidence. He was still very private about his sexuality.

He realized that much of his lack of confidence came from hiding that side of his life from people, including friends and family members, he wrote in his autobiography. Slowly, he began to come out as gay to his loved ones and people close to him. Not everyone welcomed the news, but many of the people he told already guessed that he was gay. He did not make the announcement public, and his family and friends respected his wishes to keep his sexuality to themselves. His parents were slow at first to accept his sexuality. Neil later explained in his autobiography that they came to realize, however, that he was the same person he had always been and that their relationship hadn't changed. The Harris family remained loving and close.

CHOOSING DIFFERENT ROLES

Harris took several small guest roles on a wide variety of television shows, even while his own show was still on the air. He was a fan of science fiction and was thrilled by the chance to appear in a 1993 episode of the time-travel show *Quantum Leap* shortly before *Doogie Howser, M.D.* ended. He played a very macho fraternity member opposite the show's main character Dr. Sam Beckett, played by Scott Bakula. Later in 1993, he appeared in an episode of the mystery program *Murder, She Wrote*. He played a young aspiring writer accused of murder who is assisted by the mystery writer Jessica Fletcher, played by Angela Lansbury. Other roles came later, including a guest appearance in another science fiction show called *The Outer Limits* (1996), in which he played a mentally challenged young man. He had an opportunity to play a murderer on the critically-acclaimed police drama *Homicide: Life on the Street* (1997). Such varied roles gave him a chance to show his versatile acting skills.

Many of his roles following the end of *Doogie Howser, M.D.* were in TV movies. Most of those projects received very little notice from critics. One that stood out was an adaptation of the classic Willa Cather novel *My Antonia* (1995). He played Jimmy Burden, who narrates the story of a farm community in Nebraska in the 1890s and the hardships faced by the title character, who is the daughter of recent emigrants from Europe.

He took a few film roles, as well. In the gritty drama *Animal Room* (1995) he played a teenage drug user who was placed in a disciplinary program at his high school, where he was targeted by a dangerous bully. Harris played an officer in the science fiction space adventure *Starship Troopers* (1997). He had a role alongside pop star Madonna in the romantic comedy *The Next Best Thing* (2000) and a part in the crime spoof *Undercover Brother* (2002).

Harris also starred in another television series in 1999 called *Stark Raving Mad*. The comedy featured him as a book editor trying to help his star writer, played by Tony Shaloub, overcome writer's block. The show did not find an audience and was canceled in 2000 after only twenty-two episodes aired.

REDISCOVERING THE STAGE

In 1997, Harris was cast as a member of the touring company of the hit Broadway musical *Rent*. It followed the interconnected lives of a group of struggling actors and artists trying to break out in their respective fields, touching on issues such as the AIDS epidemic and drug use. Harris played Mark, a documentary video maker. The challenging role called for him to act, sing, and dance. The touring company that Harris joined won praise from critics and audiences.

In 2001, he acted in a Broadway revival of the dark musical *Sweeney Todd: The Demon Barber of Fleet Street* about a barber who goes on a murderous rampage by killing his clients. Harris played Tobias Ragg, a former apprentice barber who finally kills the title character.

Harris was widely praised for his performance as the emcee in a 2003 Broadway revival of the dark musical *Cabaret*, which showed the nightclub life in the German city of Berlin as the Nazis were coming to power before World War II.

The theater world came to appreciate Harris's versatility. He starred in a 2004 Broadway production of the musical *Assassins!* in a dual role,

Harris (*center*) performs at a charity event alongside Mario Cantone (*left*) and Michael Cerveris (*right*), two of his costars from the musical *Assassins!*

playing the Balladeer, who weaves together the stories of several infamous murderers, and also Lee Harvey Oswald, who assassinated President John F. Kennedy. The success of Harris's work in theater kept him in the public eye even as some of his television and film projects struggled.

The Broadway roles were a great boost to Harris's career. While he was performing in musicals, he also met his future husband, fellow actor David Burtka. The two men quickly formed a close bond that soon blossomed into a romance.

CHAPTER 3

A MAN OF MANY TALENTS

Harris's willingness to try different kinds of roles and break away from his image as a teen star made him an actor with whom many writers and directors wanted to work. He earned praise for his acting roles in the years after *Doogie Howser, M.D.* ended. Another big television role, several prominent hosting jobs, and a willingness to parody his own image would help him become an even bigger star.

A DIFFERENT KIND OF CHARACTER

In 2005, he was cast for a role on an adventurous comedy sitcom called *How I Met Your Mother*. The show focused on a group of friends living in New York City. Harris was friends with Megan Brennan, who was the casting director for the show and made decisions about who to hire for various roles. She invited him to audition for the sitcom, he related in his autobiography. Harris didn't think that he had much of a chance at winning a role on the show. He tried out for the part of the outrageous character Barney Stinson. According to his autobiography, he went into the audition feeling free to take risks and went through a scene in which he played laser tag, knocking over some furniture as he put himself fully in the role. He was chosen for the part.

As a character, Barney Stinson was very different from Doogie Howser. Stinson was a selfish and immoral businessman who was always chasing after different women. Proud and vain, he dressed in suits and was always opinionated. The character eventually became more mature as the show went on, though Barney Stinson continued to brag about his dating success and his laser tag skills.

How I Met Your Mother became a major hit, airing for 208 episodes on CBS from 2005 to 2014, according to the Internet Movie Database. Critics praised the sharp storytelling, strong characters, and skilled performances. Harris's talented costars

How I Met Your Mother costars (*from left to right*) Alyson Hannigan, Neil Patrick Harris, Josh Radnor, and Jason Segel act out a scene in a 2012 episode.

included Alyson Hannigan, Jason Segel, Josh Radnor, Cristin Milioti, and Cobie Smulders. Many celebrities such as Britney Spears had small guest appearances. Other actors also had short runs on the series, sometimes coming back later in the show. Among the ensemble cast, Harris's performance as Barney Stinson was seen by many critics as the show's breakout role. The character's catchphrases and over-the-top mannerisms appealed to audiences.

Harris was nominated for several awards during the long run of the show, including Primetime Emmy Awards, People's Choice Awards, and Golden Globe Awards. He won People's Choice Awards for Favorite TV Comedy Actor in 2010 and 2012, as well as the Critic's Choice Television Award for Best Supporting Actor in a Comedy Series in 2011.

PLAYING NEIL PATRICK HARRIS

Harris has always been willing to joke about his public image, even creating a ridiculous parody of himself for a 2009 episode of the sketch comedy show *Saturday Night Live*. He had an unlikely but important cameo role in the comedy film *Harold & Kumar Go to White Castle* (2004). Harris played an exaggerated and maniacal version of himself. The movie became a cult hit and led to two sequels, *Harold & Kumar Escape from Guantanamo Bay* and *A Very Harold & Kumar 3D Christmas*, with Harris appearing as himself in both.

Harris told *CinemaBlend* that he didn't initially sign up to appear in the sequels, although he felt obligated to appear in the second film because the first one had given his career a boost. He agreed to do the third movie because he thought the idea of doing a Christmas movie with the same cast of characters was hilarious, he said in the *CinemaBlend* story.

COMING OUT

By the time *How I Met Your Mother* had started airing on CBS, attitudes toward LGBTQ people had shifted. Society was more accepting of people attracted to the same gender than when Harris had been growing up. Harris remained very private about his life away from the cameras and off stage. His family, friends, and the people he worked with knew that he was gay. He had not taken the step of making the news public. That changed in 2006, when he publicly declared his sexuality in a 2006 statement to *People* magazine: "I am happy to dispel any rumors or misconceptions and am quite proud to say that I am a very content gay man living my life to the fullest and feel most fortunate to be working with wonderful people in the business I love."

Harris came out publicly for several reasons. There had been rumors that he was gay, though he never confirmed them publicly. Before his announcement, other rumors were circulating that he had denied being gay. He wanted to correct the record so that no one thought he was trying to hide his sexuality.

> "
> I am happy to dispel any rumors or misconceptions and am quite proud to say that I am a very content gay man living my life to the fullest and feel most fortunate to be working with wonderful people in the business I love."
>
> —NEIL PATRICK HARRIS

41

In 2009, Harris received a Streamy Award for Best Male Actor in a Comedy Web Series for his work on the internet miniseries *Dr. Horrible's Sing-Along Blog.*

STREAMY AWARDS.

He had also met his future husband, David Burtka, in 2004, while both were appearing in musicals. A mutual friend had introduced them, and Harris was attracted right away to Burtka. Burtka was in a relationship at the time that they met and was helping his then-boyfriend raise twins. Harris and Burtka got together after Burtka and his then-boyfriend split up. The two were already in a serious, committed relationship when Harris made his announcement. He didn't want to disrespect Burtka or make him feel as though he wasn't important.

The announcement that he was gay did nothing to slow Harris's career. Audiences continued to tune in to *How I Met Your Mother*.

CHALLENGING ROLES

Neil Patrick Harris has continually chosen parts in plays, movies, and as a program host that have demonstrated his range as a performer. Even while he was working on *How I Met Your Mother*, he was taking on other projects that included films, theatrical roles, and stints as the host of widely watched awards shows.

One of his quirkier roles was as the star of the musical miniseries *Dr. Horrible's Sing-Along Blog* (2008), a web-based show created by television writer and director Joss Whedon, his brothers Jed and Zack Whedon, and writer Maurissa Tancharoen. Harris played Dr. Horrible, an evil scientist who wanted to become a supervillain. Dr. Horrible was attempting to join an organization called the Evil League of Evil by committing cartoonishly evil acts. The show was a hit with audiences and critics. It received several awards, including Best Male Actor in a Comedy Award Series for Harris at the 2009 Streamy Awards for web-based shows. It also won a 2009 Creative Arts Emmy Award for

Harris shares the screen with the animated characters Clumsy, Brainy, Smurfette, Gutsy, and Papa Smurf in a scene from the hit movie *The Smurfs*.

Outstanding Special Class–Short-format Live-Action Entertainment Programs.

Harris has provided voices for numerous characters in animated shows and films. In *Cloudy with a Chance of Meatballs* (2009), he voices a monkey named Steve who is the friend and lab assistant of main character Flint Lockwood, who has invented a machine that makes food fall from the sky. Steve "speaks" through a device around his neck.

In *The Smurfs* (2011), Harris plays Patrick

Winslow, a young man who encounters the small blue title creatures shortly after they are magically transported to New York City. Patrick and his wife, Grace (played by Jayma Mays), become friends with the Smurfs and help them return to their own world. The Smurfs help the couple realize that they are ready to start a family of their own.

The Smurfs and *Cloudy with a Chance of Meatballs* were both hits with audiences and inspired sequels. He reprised his voice work as Steve in *Cloudy with a Chance of Meatballs 2*

(2013) and again starred as Patrick in *The Smurfs 2* (2013), both of which were successful box office hits.

From 2010 to 2015, he appeared in three episodes of *The Penguins of Madagascar*, an animated series that followed the lives of a group of penguins living in the Central Park Zoo in New York City. Harris was the voice for Dr. Blowhole, who was an evil mad scientist and the sworn enemy of the penguins.

Harris briefly had his own puppet show called *Neil's Puppet Dreams*. The web series aired for seven episodes in 2012 and 2013 on The Nerdist Channel. Cocreated with the help of his boyfriend and future husband, David Burtka, the quirky show imagines that Harris dreams in puppets. Each episode begins with Harris falling asleep and features a different dream populated by marionettes from The Jim Henson Company. Dreaming Neil encounters many uncomfortable situations, such as visiting the doctor and getting abducted by extraterrestrials. The series was nominated for a 2013 Webby Award for "Best Comedy: Long Form or Series."

Harris had mixed results with his more mature film roles following the end of *How I Met Your Mother.* He had a supporting role in the poorly received comedic western *A Million Ways to Die in the West* (2014). Harris had more success playing a creepy villain in the movie thriller *Gone Girl* (2014), which was based on a novel of the same name by Gillian Flynn. Harris's character, Desi Collings, is the former boyfriend of main character Amy Dunne, played by Rosamund

Pike. Amy goes to Desi for help while she's hiding out from her husband. Under the pretense of helping her, Desi holds her prisoner until she escapes from him. The film was popular with critics and audiences.

TAKING THE STAGE

Harris has stayed involved in musicals when his schedule has allowed him the time. He made his theatrical directorial debut in 2010 when he led a production of *Rent* staged for a weekend at the Hollywood Bowl. The production featured his friend Vanessa Hudgens in the lead role as Mimi, a dancer living with HIV.

In 2011, he directed a drama called *The Expert at the Card Table* in Los Angeles, earning rave reviews for the small play about a magician revealing the secrets to how card tricks work to his audience.

Harris took the stage himself in 2011 as Bobby in a concert production of the beloved Stephen Sondheim musical *Company* with the New York Philharmonic providing musical backing. In the musical, Harris's character is an unmarried man who both wants to find love and fears commitment, even as his friends get married, get divorced, and form new relationships.

In 2014, he took the starring role in an edgy musical drama called *Hedwig and the Angry Inch*. Harris's character, Hedwig, is the lead singer of a rock band who has undergone a sex change operation and is making a living playing music in dingy bars. Based on a 2001 movie of the same name, the musical tells the story of how a former lover stole all her songs before going on to become a major star. The demanding role called for Harris to dress in elaborate stage makeup and costumes, sing, and dance nightly. Harris played the role convincingly and the show was a major success on Broadway. His work as Hedwig earned him a 2014 Tony Award for Best Actor in a Musical.

His wide range of skills, from singing to stage magic, have made Harris a popular choice to host televised awards shows. He has hosted the Tony Awards four times, in 2009, 2011, 2012, and 2013. He hosted the Primetime Emmy Awards in 2009 and 2013. In 2015, he became the first openly gay man to host the Academy Awards. Ironically, his work as host of the Tony Awards earned him four Primetime Emmy awards in the category of Outstanding Special Class Program. He has also won a fifth Primetime Emmy Award for Outstanding Guest Actor in a Comedy Series for a 2010 guest appearance on the musical television comedy-drama *Glee*.

MORE HIT SHOWS

Harris has stayed busy in television since *How I Met Your Mother* ended in 2014. He took a small role in the series *American Horror Story: Freak Show* (2015) as Chester Creb, a creepy magician in a traveling carnival.

For the title role in the Broadway production of *Hedwig and the Angry Inch*, Harris had to act, sing, and wear daring costumes for every performance.

Harris began starring in another quirky series in 2017, this time a streaming show for Netflix. Based on a popular series of young adult books by Lemony Snicket (the pen name for author Daniel Handler), *A Series of Unfortunate Events* tells the story of the orphaned Baudelaire siblings, Violet and Klaus, whose parents are killed in a suspicious accident. The young children are sent to live with their closest living relative, the evil Count Olaf, played by Harris. Count Olaf only wants to cheat them out of the fortune their parents left to them.

The show was well-received by critics and praised for its handling of themes such as grief and loss. Harris was nominated for a 2018 Satellite Award for Best Actor in a Series—Comedy or Musical for his work as Count Olaf in the second season. A third season that would complete the adaptations of Handler's books is planned for release in 2019.

Popular with audiences, Harris has said that he was approached to take over hosting duties for CBS's *The Late Show* formerly hosted by David Letterman and *The Late Late Show*, formerly hosted by Craig Ferguson. Harris declined both opportunities to host the popular talk shows because he felt he would get bored doing the same type of show every night, according to a 2014 *Rolling Stone* article by Cory Grow.

Harris created his own hosting opportunity in 2017 with the children's game show *Genius Junior*. First airing in 2018, the show features Harris as a

Harris's charm and sense of showmanship make him a natural fit to host awards ceremonies, such as the God's Love We Deliver Golden Heart Awards in 2016.

host quizzing teams of children twelve years old and younger on subjects such as math, spelling, geography, and memory skills. Questions get harder as the game continues. Winners receive cash prizes, while runners-up get trips to places like Washington, DC. Harris told *Variety* that he enjoys hosting the show because it highlights the abilities of exceptional children and challenges viewers to test their own knowledge.

CHAPTER 4

A THEATRICAL YOUTH

David Michael Burtka was born on May 29, 1975, in Dearborn, Michigan, just outside Detroit. His parents, Deborah Zajas and Daniel Burtka, raised him in the nearby town of Canton, Michigan, alongside his older sister, Jennifer. His father was a special education teacher and his mother worked as a secretary.

Family meals were a big part of their lives, and the Burtkas regularly hosted or attended large gatherings focused around food. Those family get-togethers helped young David become interested in cooking and preparing meals. He described his family's connection with food in an interview with *Spoon University:*

> We would cook like crazy! There would be a different family party every weekend, we would go to someone's house and everyone would bring a dish to pass around, there would be three different proteins and eight different side dishes and seven different desserts. Food was what we based all of our memories around.

FINDING A PASSION

As a boy, David was part of a Detroit-area theater group for children called the Peanut Butter Players. They put on family-friendly plays and musicals such as *The Wizard of Oz; You're a Good Man, Charlie Brown;* and *Tom Sawyer.*

When he was eleven years old, David was cast in a Peanut Butter Players production of *Peter Pan* as one of the Darling kids who fly to Never-Never Land with Peter Pan. During one performance, the harness that held him up in the air so that it looked like he was flying broke, causing him to fall. He was unharmed by the fall, though he had

> "There would be a different family party every weekend, we would go to someone's house and everyone would bring a dish to pass around ... Food was what we based all of our memories around."
>
> —DAVID BURTKA

to go to the emergency room to be checked out and missed a few days of performances, according to a *Playbill* story by Seth Rudetsky.

David attended Plymouth Salem High School. The school featured a strong performing arts program for students interested in theater. David was quickly drawn to the program, he told *Pride Source*. Friendly and easy to get along with, David was accepted by many older students. It helped that his sister, Jennifer, was popular, well-liked, and a star athlete. She helped him make friends and fit in with her set

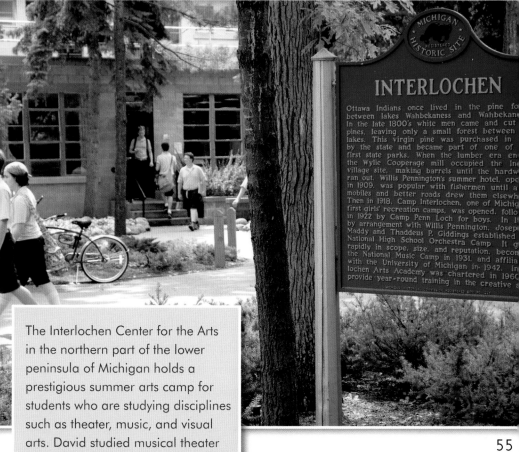

INTERLOCHEN

Ottawa Indians once lived in the pine fo between lakes Wahbekaness and Wahbekan In the late 1800's white men came and cut pines, leaving only a small forest between lakes. This virgin pine was purchased in by the state and became part of one of first state parks. When the lumber era en the Wylie Cooperage mill occupied the In village site, making barrels until the hardw ran out. Willis Pennington's summer hotel, ope in 1909, was popular with fishermen until a mobiles and better roads drew them elsewh Then in 1918, Camp Interlochen, one of Michig first girls' recreation camps, was opened, follo in 1922 by Camp Penn Loch for boys. In 1 by arrangement with Willis Pennington, Josep Maddy and Thaddeus P. Giddings established National High School Orchestra Camp It g rapidly in scope, size, and reputation, becon the National Music Camp in 1931, and affilia with the University of Michigan in 1942. In lochen Arts Academy was chartered in 1960 provide year-round training in the creative a

The Interlochen Center for the Arts in the northern part of the lower peninsula of Michigan holds a prestigious summer arts camp for students who are studying disciplines such as theater, music, and visual arts. David studied musical theater and dance for three summers there.

of friends. He became one of the popular students who hung out together just outside school grounds in a place called "The Pit," he told *Pride Source*.

David's interest in the theater intensified. He won many lead roles in school plays. His gifts as an actor were obvious, and his parents encouraged him to pursue his love of theater. He spent three summers studying dance and musical theater at the prestigious Interlochen Center for the Arts in Grand Traverse County, Michigan. There, he was able to refine his skills and try new things on stage. At his high school, he stood out because of his interest in theater and his dramatic skills. At Interlochen, he was interacting with other young students who were similarly talented. He graduated from Plymouth Salem High School in 1993.

PURSUING THE DREAM

Burtka enrolled in the University of Michigan in Ann Arbor in 1993. He majored in musical theater in the university's School of Music, Theatre & Dance. He continued to grow as an actor through his participation in the highly-regarded Musical Theatre program. In his spare time, he discovered that he enjoyed cooking, he told *Pride Source*. He often made meals for his friends after finding recipes he liked in magazines and cookbooks. Burtka saw it as a challenge to take ingredients and turn them into delicious dishes that his friends enjoyed.

Burtka came out as gay to his family while he was in college, according to an interview with his father for *Oprah's Next Chapter*. He had realized he was gay from an early age and had looked up to gay artists such as Keith Haring, an edgy painter and graffiti artist who died as a result of HIV/AIDS in 1990. His family was very supportive.

The University of Michigan in Ann Arbor has a well-regarded theater program that attracted Burtka. Other acclaimed actors who received an education there include James Earl Jones.

Burtka graduated with a bachelor of fine arts degree in Musical Theatre in 1997. Shortly after graduating, he moved to New York City to start looking for opportunities to act. Many young actors who want to start their theater careers move to New York City, where there are many opportunities to get noticed in all types of roles. The competition is fierce, even for actors as skilled as Burtka. He spent more time strengthening his skills.

MAKING A LIVING THROUGH COMMERCIALS

As a young actor looking for opportunities to break through in show business, David acted in television commercials for a wide variety of companies, brands, and organizations. In an ad for Old Navy, he danced with company spokeswoman Morgan Fairchild and the famous drag queen RuPaul. He did commercials for the Midwestern soft drink company Faygo, as well as for GAP, and for a Michigan initiative promoting safe sex. One of his commercials was for the United States Army. That intense ad took ten days to shoot and required Burtka to go through a day of army boot camp. Burtka has since appeared in advertising campaigns for companies such as the clothing brand London Fog and the financial services company Capital One.

He went to the William Esper Studio in Manhattan for more theatrical training. The well-regarded drama school specializes in teaching students the Meisner Technique, which emphasizes emotional realism and opening actors up to help them react naturally within the imaginary scenarios of stage productions. He also took dance classes at Broadway Dance Center on the Upper West Side.

GETTING ROLES

Burtka worked hard to get theatrical roles in New York City, where he competed against many other talented actors. Shortly after moving there he took a small role in a production of a biblical musical called *Children of Eden* in 1997. The two-act musical is a family-friendly retelling of the first nine chapters of the *Book of Genesis*.

He followed *Children of Eden* with roles in the New York production of a pair of off-Broadway musicals. He was in the satirical rock-and-roll musical *Bad Boy Johnny*, as well as *Beautiful Thing*, which told the story of two teenage boys falling in love with each other.

He was also cast in the touring company for the Broadway musical *Beauty and the Beast*, which ran until March 1999 and visited cities such as St. Louis, Missouri; Detroit, Michigan; and Minneapolis, Minnesota. He played the parts of Salt and Pepper, a pair of salt and pepper shakers brought to life by magic.

David Burtka (*left*) appears alongside his costars (*from left to right*) Marian Seldes, Brian Murray, and Kathleen Early on opening night of the edgy drama *The Play About the Baby* in 2001.

A different kind of opportunity came along in 1999, when Burtka was chosen for a part in the gay comedy-romance film *24 Nights*. Burtka plays Toby, the object of affection for a man named Jonathan (played by Kevin Isola), who believes Toby is the answer to his Christmas wish to find true love. The movie was not widely released in theaters. It was shown at a few film festivals where it was warmly received by audiences and honored with several awards.

Burtka's major theatrical breakthrough came in 2000, when he appeared as the male lead in the challenging, avant-garde Edward Albee play *The Play About the Baby*. The edgy play depicts the relationship between a young couple called Boy, played by Burtka, and Girl, played by Rebecca Harris.

Burtka's acting in the role was highly praised. He received a Clarence Derwent Award from the Foundation of Actors' Equity in 2001 for the role. In 2002, he made his Broadway debut as a member of the replacement cast in another Albee play called *The Goat, or Who is Sylvia?* The bizarre play tells the story of a man who is in love with a goat named Sylvia.

He continued to try new directions with the roles he chose. Burtka took his first role in a television show in 2002. He appeared as an intern in an episode of the political drama *The West Wing* (2002). Later, he would have a small part in the crime drama *Crossing Jordan* (2005). Both appearances were for only a single episode, but they broadened his experience.

EARNING A PLACE ON BROADWAY

The years of hard work and good reviews finally paid off for Burtka in 2003. He was chosen for a role in the 2003 revival production of the Broadway musical *Gypsy*, featuring lyrics by Stephen Sondheim. The musical was first staged in 1959. It was inspired by the life of a flamboyant actress, striptease artist, and entertainer named Gypsy Rose Lee. It focuses on Lee's relationship with her controlling mother, Rose. In the musical,

Actress Kate Reinders celebrates with Burtka after opening night of the 2003 revival of the musical Gypsy. Reinders played June, who ran off with Burtka's character, Tulsa.

Rose dreams of managing her two daughters, June and Louise, to successful careers on stage. The character Louise is based on Gypsy Rose Lee, while that of June is based on her sister.

Burtka was given the role of Tulsa, a singer who becomes part of a stage show starring June. He and June run away and get married, leaving Rose to manage Louise in whatever venues she can find, including burlesque halls. The production Burtka joined was the first Broadway revival of the show since 1989. It featured Broadway legend Bernadette Peters as Rose.

The revival of *Gypsy* was a major success. Burtka's performance as Tulsa received positive reviews and gave his career a boost. His singing can be heard on the Broadway revival cast recording of the musical.

Burtka first met Neil Patrick Harris through a mutual friend while he was in *Gypsy*. Though it would be a while before they started dating, they ran into each other several times after that first meeting. Burtka, who was in a relationship at the time with the actor, director, and producer Lane Janger, was unaware that Harris was attracted to him, Burtka later wrote in a joint article with Harris in *Out* magazine. As they kept meeting, a bond formed between them.

CHAPTER 5

CHANGING DIRECTIONS

B urtka was determined to build on his Broadway success from *Gypsy* with roles in theater and in Hollywood. *Gypsy* had been very successful, with 451 performances staged between the time the show opened on May 1, 2003, and its closing on May 30, 2004. The show was nominated for four 2003 Tony Awards, including Best Revival of a Musical. For Burtka, the show was an opportunity to be seen and heard by audiences every night. He hoped that his work in the show could lead to other prominent roles.

RAISING TWINS

Burtka had been dating Lane Janger for several years during the late 1990s and early 2000s. They had twin children, a boy named Javin and a girl named Flynn, who were born to a surrogate mother in 2000. Biologically, the children were Janger's. Burtka's mother was also delighted and was always asking for pictures and updates.

Burtka helped raise the twins until they were three-and-a-half years old. By that time, his relationship with Janger had become rocky. They were still together when Burtka and Harris first met, but the relationship was in serious trouble by that time. Burtka and Janger finally broke up in 2004. Even after the breakup, Burtka remained involved in the twins' lives.

ORIGINATING A ROLE

Burtka followed *Gypsy* by taking a part in the new musical *The Opposite of Sex* in 2004. The musical was based on a 1998 movie that was not a musical and had featured Christina Ricci, Lisa Kudrow, and Johnny Gorecki in starring roles. The dark comedy told the story of a teenage girl who moves in with her gay half-brother and becomes attracted to his boyfriend. She and the boyfriend have an affair and she gets pregnant. The movie had not been a huge hit with audiences at the box office.

The musical *The Opposite of Sex* was based on an absurd 1998 hit comedy of the same name that promised to amuse and offend its audience.

Burtka played the role of Matt, a sexually confused character, in the musical's 2004 premiere in San Francisco and in its 2006 East Coast premiere in Williamstown, Massachusetts. Unlike *Gypsy*, he couldn't look at how other performers had acted in the role for inspiration. By originating the role, he had to work closely with the musical's directors to work out how Matt would be portrayed on stage.

Burtka was praised by critics for his singing in the role, though *The Opposite of Sex* itself received mixed reviews. The show had an extended run in San Francisco through October 2004. It also had a short run from August 9 to August 20, 2006, at the Williamstown Theatre Festival in New Jersey, although an expected Broadway opening never took place.

TURNING TO TV

Burtka started doing more work in Hollywood in the mid-2000s, often taking small parts in TV shows or starring in made-for-TV movies. He moved to Los Angeles to find more work and to continue his budding relationship with Harris. They eventually bought a house together in California.

Harris had once again become a television star, on *How I Met Your Mother*. Burtka also took a small role on the show. He played Scooter, the old high school boyfriend of one of the main characters, Lily Aldrin, played by Alyson Hannigan. Scooter appears in seven episodes of the show. The character never got over being dumped by Lily at their senior prom. Scooter has many quirks, including a dream of becoming a baseball umpire. At one point he becomes a waiter because he thinks doing so will help him win Lily's heart.

In 2007, Burtka began working on a reality show called *On the Lot*. The show was produced by DreamWorks Television and developed by renowned director Steven Spielberg. The reality program began with eighteen aspiring movie directors competing against one another to sign a development deal with DreamWorks Studios. At the beginning of the show, each of the eighteen contestants had to put together a short film screened for a panel of judges that included, at different times, actress Carrie Fisher and directors Wes Craven and Brad Silberling. Audience members would vote on their favorite films and the lowest vote-getters would eventually be cut from the show.

Burtka was one of the actors who starred in some of the short films made for the show. He had parts in thirteen of the show's episodes in shorts with titles like *Army Guy* and *Open House*. Such roles gave him more chances to show off his versatility as an actor.

On the Lot turned out to be an expensive failure. The show had originally been set up to be broadcast five nights a week, but was cut down to once weekly to reduce expenses. Audiences were not drawn to the short films or the show's glimpses inside the filmmaking process. It was canceled after the first season because of its cost and low ratings.

Burtka was becoming dissatisfied with acting, he told *Page Six*. He wasn't working enough in shows or films to have a major career breakthrough. There also weren't as many opportunities in the theater in California. He and Harris had worked out a long-distance relationship early on when they were first together, but they didn't want to be apart again. Burtka began considering a career shift.

TRAGEDY AND CHANGE

In 2009, Burtka's mother, Deborah, was diagnosed with leukemia. She died twenty days after the diagnosis. The illness and the speed of her decline were shocking. As soon as they received the news of her illness, Burtka and Harris went to Michigan so that they could be with Deborah and with the rest of Burtka's family.

His mother's death made Burtka think more deeply about a career change, he told *Montecristo Magazine*. He had enjoyed cooking

> "It's been a long road. A humble Dearborn beginning ... Eventually I moved to LA but, not good for me, I felt rejected. So I stopped acting and, needing to feel good inside, became a chef."
>
> —DAVID BURTKA

since college and continued honing his skills. He decided that he wanted to make a change by becoming a professional chef, he told *Page Six*. He enrolled in cooking classes at Le Cordon Bleu in Pasadena, California. Le Cordon Bleu is one of the world's best-known schools for learning the culinary arts, with locations around the world.

Students undergo long and intense days of training as they work toward their goals. As he told *Page Six* in a 2015 interview:

> It's been a long road. A humble Dearborn beginning. Secretary mom, dad teaching handicapped children. Working for what they had. Eventually I moved to LA but, not good for me, I felt rejected. So I stopped acting and, needing to feel good inside, became a chef.

THE CELEBRITY CHEF

Since finishing his training at Le Cordon Bleu, Burtka has made several appearances as a celebrity judge on cooking shows. He can bring the perspective of someone who appreciates complex flavors and who understands how much hard work it is to prepare good food to these judging panels. He and Harris made a joint appearance as judges for an episode of *Iron Chef America* (2013). Burtka served as a judge and mentor on a 2015 episode of *Beat Bobby Flay*, in which aspiring chefs try to outcook celebrity chef Bobby Flay. He made appearances on the cooking show *The Kitchen* in 2015 and 2017, and he was a judge on final episode of the 2018 season of *Worst Cooks in America.*

Burtka graduated from Le Cordon Bleu in 2009 with a degree in culinary arts. In 2010, he started a catering business with his classmate Molly Hanissee. They called the business Gourmet M.D.—the "M.D." representing the initials of their first names—and set out to cater events for Hollywood stars and studios. Their catering clients included Christina Hendricks and Jon Hamm from the popular show *Mad Men*, *Star Trek* actor Zack Quinto, and *American Idol* judge Kara DioGuardi.

Burtka gives a cooking demonstration in 2016 as part of the Food Network & Cooking Channel South Beach Wine & Food Festival, held in Miami Beach, Florida.

BACK IN SHOW BUSINESS

Culinary school and helping to run Gourmet M.D. had been a welcome break from performing for Burtka. He still took some acting roles. He had a role as an outrageous, fictionalized version of himself alongside Harris in *A Very Harold & Kumar 3D Christmas* (2011). He started acting again on a regular basis in 2012.

Burtka was in all seven episodes of Harris's off-kilter comedy series *Neil's Puppet Dreams.* He played himself in those shows, appearing in the framing scenes before and after the dreams and sometimes in the dreams themselves.

He had another film role in the movie *Dance-Off* (2014), about a pair of rival competitive dance teams. The family-oriented movie was released directly to streaming services without appearing in theaters. Burtka plays JT, the well-meaning son of the woman organizing the dance competition.

Burtka returned to Broadway in April 2015 in the musical *It Shoulda Been You.* He was one of the leads in the comedy about two families coming together for a wedding. Directed by actor David Hyde Pierce, the musical was a hit with audiences and played for 135 regular performances. Unfortunately, Burtka had to go on medical leave for the last month because of vocal issues and missed the show's closing.

Burtka also made small guest appearances in the shows *American Horror Story* and *A Series of Unfortunate Events*. In the *A Series of*

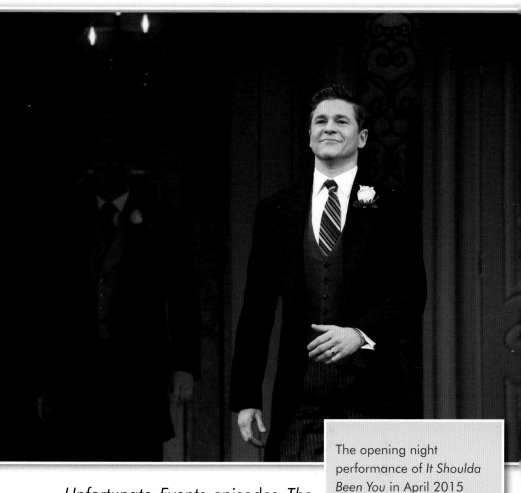

Unfortunate Events episodes *The Carnivorous Carnival: Part 1* and *The Carnivorous Carnival: Part 2* (2018), he played an audience member. The couples' twin children were also in the scene, bringing the entire family together.

The opening night performance of *It Shoulda Been You* in April 2015 marked Burtka's return to Broadway after many years spent working on other types of projects.

CHAPTER 6

A MAGICAL LIFE TOGETHER

Harris and Burtka are among the most prominent same-sex couples in the country. They have spent much of their relationship in the public eye, while making time for each other and to raise a family. They have remained busy and successful in their professional lives. Their devotion to each other is also clear in their public appearances together.

THE FIRST MEETING

Harris and Burtka first met in 2004 through a mutual actress friend while Harris was working on *Cabaret* and Burtka was in *Gypsy*. Harris was instantly drawn to Burtka, who was still seeing Janger at the time. He thought that Burtka must be their female friend's boyfriend. When he asked her about him later, she told him that Burtka was gay and that he was in a relationship, the couple shared in an article they wrote together for *Out* magazine.

Burtka's reaction in their first meeting was different. He already knew that Harris had played Doogie Howser. He had only watched the show a couple times and he acted unimpressed. He did think it would be nice to know Harris and introduced himself, as revealed in the *Out* story. Burtka was still seeing Janger and never expected that he and Harris would be in a relationship.

Harris, who was single at the time, arranged to be at places with his actress friend when Burtka would also be around. They hung out together at an *American Idol* viewing party, where Harris was nervous around him. Sometimes they would have lunch together, alongside people they knew. Gradually they became acquainted and became comfortable around each other.

Burtka and Janger broke up later in 2004. A week after the breakup, Harris and Burtka went on their first date together. They saw the Angelina Jolie crime drama *Taking Lives*. After that, they started seeing each other every night, calling each other several times each day, and sending numerous text messages back and forth. In an interview with *Out* magazine, Harris explained how their personalities

Burtka and Harris walked the red carpet for the first time as a couple at the Fifty-Ninth Primetime Emmy Awards in September 2007.

meshed: "I tend to weigh options before making decisions, and David is the polar opposite of that. We're hyper similar and also incredibly opposite."

BUILDING A LIFE

Burtka and Harris had both been renting apartments in New York City while working on their theater projects. They moved into a house in California's San Fernando Valley in 2006. Harris had taken Burtka out to meet friends and the cast and crew of *How I Met Your Mother*, but the couple had not been officially out together in California.

The pair attended the 2007 Primetime Emmy Awards ceremony as a couple. Harris later confirmed his relationship with Burtka while he was a guest on the *Ellen DeGeneres Show*. It was their first official appearance together and happened shortly after Burtka proposed to Harris, on the same street corner where they had first met in 2004. Harris said yes. The next year, Harris proposed to Burtka, as they related in *Out*.

> I tend to weigh options before making decisions, and David is the polar opposite of that. We're hyper similar and also incredibly opposite."
> —NEIL PATRICK HARRIS

The couple continued talking about having children, eventually agreeing that they wanted kids while their own parents would still be able to enjoy them. Burtka's mother was diagnosed with cancer

As devoted parents, Harris and Burtka have shared many adventures, including boat rides, with their twin children, Harper and Gideon.

in 2008. Her death shortly after gave them a sense of urgency. They decided to become parents through a surrogate, according to Harris's autobiography.

Their twins, son Gideon Scott and daughter Harper Grace, were born in October 2010. One twin is biologically Harris's and the other is Burtka's. They decided that they didn't want to know which one is which, so that they would be sure to treat them equally.

BACK TO THE EAST COAST

Burtka and Harris moved their family back to New York City in 2014, shortly after the final season of *How I Met Your Mother* ended. They had enjoyed living in California, but always planned to return to New York, Harris recounted in his autobiography. They even kept an apartment in the city for when they needed to visit. Before the move, they bought

HALLOWEEN FUN

For David Burtka and Neil Patrick Harris, Halloween is a wildly creative family production. Every year, the pair and their children dress up in themed costumes. In 2011, when the twins were a year old, Burtka dressed up as Peter Pan, Harris as Captain Hook, and Harper and Gideon as Tinkerbell and Smee. In 2012, Harper dressed up as Dorothy, with the rest of her family playing her *Wizard of Oz* companions. Subsequent years have included themes such as *Alice in Wonderland*, superheroes and supervillains, *Star Wars*, and carnival performers. In 2016, the family paid tribute to classic Hollywood, with Harris as Groucho Marx, Burtka as Charlie Chaplin, Gideon as James Dean, and Harper as Marilyn Monroe.

a home in the Harlem neighborhood of Upper Manhattan in 2013 and spent more than a year renovating it.

The five-story home had been a bed-and-breakfast and needed a lot of work before the family could move in. The changes they made included updating the kitchen to expand the cooking space and adding a secret room with a hidden door that Neil could use to store his collection of magic memorabilia. Another space was set aside for gatherings and entertaining guests.

Harris and Burtka were guests at the Twenty-Second Annual Elton John AIDS Foundation Academy Awards Viewing Party, held in March 2014. John is pictured between Harris and Burtka.

Burtka and Harris had decided to get married when the Marriage Equality Act was passed in New York State in 2011, according to Elizabeth Leonard in *People*. They had already proposed to each other and exchanged engagement rings years before. In September 2014, they traveled to Italy and were married in a ceremony they kept secret from everyone but their family and friends. The ceremony was officiated by Pam Fryman, Harris's director on *How I Met Your Mother*. Their twins, Harper and Gideon, took part in the ceremony. Their friend, singer Elton John, performed a song for them at the reception. Harris also performed some magic tricks for the audience.

CHAPTER 7

CHANGING THE WORLD

Since making their relationship public in 2006, Harris and Burtka have been very active on LGBTQ issues. They have been vocal advocates for expanding the rights of same-sex couples, particularly on topics like marriage and adoption rights.

Harris has long been known in Hollywood for his generosity and charity work. Burtka has also contributed to many worthy causes, both alongside Harris and on his own. Together, they have shown a willingness to use their fame to push for changes that they believe would make the world a better place. In

Burtka and Harris were honored together at the L.A. Gay & Lesbian Center's Fortieth Anniversary Gala in 2011. The theme of the event was "Forty Years of Family."

many cases, they have led by setting a good example for their fans to follow.

SETTING GOOD EXAMPLES

Harris and Burtka have expressed a desire to show their twins the importance of giving back according to a *Yahoo! Entertainment* story. Harper and Gideon Burtka-Harris were born into lives of considerable wealth and privilege. Their fathers want them to be aware that not everyone is as fortunate as they are and to see that it's important to help others.

The family spends the days leading up to holidays like Thanksgiving and Christmas, and the holidays themselves, delivering meals to people in need. They work with a couple of different charities to make the meal deliveries happen.

Their other charity work includes contributions to Project Last Mile, which forms partnerships between the Coca-Cola Company and charitable organizations that work to send medical supplies to poor regions of Africa. The project uses Coca-Cola's massive logistics network to make sure medicine makes it to remote villages. They contribute to several organizations devoted to fighting cancer, including the American Cancer Society, Stand Up to Cancer, and Susan G. Komen for the Cure.

Some of their other charitable work has included contributions to Clothes Off Our Back, which holds charity auctions of clothing worn by celebrities. They

Joining young cancer survivor Luke Weber, Burtka and Harris celebrate the 2016 Cycle for Survival fundraising event in New York City.

have given to Feeding America, an organization that consists of a nationwide network of food banks, shelters, and soup kitchens dedicated to feeding the hungry.

PARENTAL DUTIES

As parents, they have worked to provide their children with a fun and stable environment where they can be themselves while learning to treat others with respect. Harper and Gideon call Burtka "Daddy" and Harris

CHAMPIONING GAY RIGHTS

Harris and Burtka have both been outspoken in their support for LGBTQ causes. They are prominent supporters of The Trevor Project, which provides suicide prevention services to LGBTQ people younger than age twenty-five. Harris and Burtka both delivered positive messages for the It Gets Better project aimed at LGBTQ youth who have been bullied because of their sexuality or gender identity. The project is intended to help prevent suicides by LGBTQ teens. Videos for the project are intended to help young people realize that other LGBTQ people have struggled with their sexuality, but that their lives did get better.

Harris also helped start the Human Rights Campaign's Americans for Marriage Equality initiative, which was established to advocate for same-sex marriage in the United States. Burtka is a contributor to the Born This Way Foundation, which was started by Lady Gaga to provide support for LGBTQ teens.

"Poppa." They do many of the same things other parents do, including getting the children ready for school, shuttling them to playdates, and making sure they do their homework before putting them to bed. Burtka explained the balance of their parenting strategies in a joint *Rolling Stone* interview:

I have very maternal instincts when it comes to kids. Neil is better at doing tasks, sometimes. But, you know, it's a good balance. Neil is ready for them to start thinking on their own and making good decisions. And I'm like, 'They can't … it doesn't work that way yet! You've gotta be patient, you've gotta hold off.'

> "I have very maternal instincts when it comes to kids. Neil is better at doing tasks … it's a good balance. Neil is ready for them to start thinking on their own and making good decisions. And I'm like, 'They can't … it doesn't work that way yet! You've gotta be patient, you've gotta hold off.'"
>
> —DAVID BURTKA

According to an *Architectural Digest* interview by Elizabeth Quinn Brown, the twins have led Harris and Burtka to make some changes in their lives, such as buying things that are made to last. They try to make everything fun by doing things like hosting mock cooking challenges for the kids and their guests. Both men place a high value on having family meals together. They have a strict rule against having toys or mobile devices at the table so that everyone can connect over their meal.

AHEAD OF THE CROWD

Burtka and Harris are both trendsetters whose personal styles have made an impact on pop culture.

Harris, Burtka, and their children take the stage at the 2018 Wigstock festival celebrating New York City's LGBTQ community. Harris was a cohost for the event.

Harris, in particular, is a frequent user of Twitter and other social media outlets. His audience of millions of followers on Twitter can read his thoughts on numerous topics, see family photos, and learn about his projects.

Several aspects of their lives together have been featured in magazines. The couple told the story of their engagement in a 2012 issue of the LGBTQ publication *Out* magazine, paired with photos of them together. *Architectural Digest* did an extensive article on their home in a feature in 2015 that focused on the renovations they carried out to make it right for their family.

Burtka's passion for good food and cooking has led him to take on several interesting projects aimed at helping people become comfortable in the kitchen. He trained as a chef at the famed Babbo Italian restaurant in New York City. The intense kitchen work was a shift from acting, but he learned to handle pressure and stick to a strict cooking process and schedule.

In 2016, he made a television special for the Food Network called *Life's a Party with David Burtka.* The show followed Burtka as he planned a surprise birthday party for his friend, actor James Carpinello. It featured him preparing dishes with help from Harper and Gideon and inviting guests such as television host Kelly Ripa and Carpinello's wife, actress Amy Acker. He followed the special by writing a cookbook called *Life Is a Party* featuring recipes, decorating tips, and advice on preparing for big events. The book is scheduled to be released in 2019.

Harris is also a published author. He wrote a best-selling autobiography titled *Neil Patrick Harris: Choose Your Own Autobiography.* Published in 2014, it follows the quirky format of the Choose Your Own Adventure book series that was popular in the 1980s. Told in the second-person, it lets the reader skip around in the narrative of Harris's life up to that point.

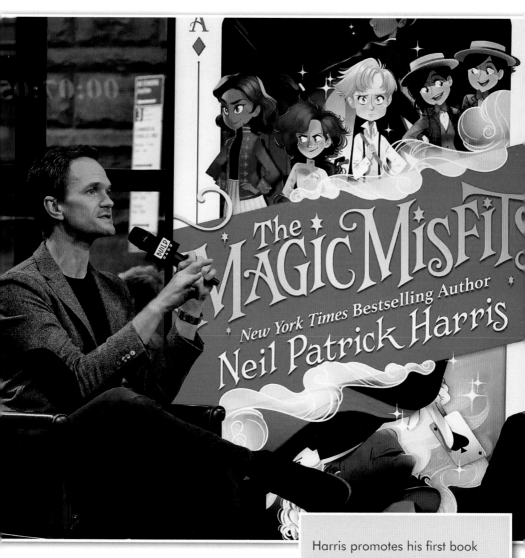

Harris promotes his first book for young readers, *The Magic Misfits*. The book and its sequels all include codes and magic tricks for his readers to learn.

Harris is also the author of children's books. His first book for young readers, *The Magic Misfits*, was released in 2017. The book tells the story of a group of kids who have to use their talents and their love of magic to defeat a group of evil carnival workers. Simple magic tricks are included in the story for readers to try. The book was well-received. The second book in the series, *The Magic Misfits: The Second Story*, was published in 2018.

Burtka and Harris have made their marks in the worlds of acting, cooking, writing, and activism. Their passion for their work has been shown by the excellence of their completed projects. As a power couple, they have influenced millions of people while working to raise their children to become loving and thoughtful people.

1973 Neil Patrick Harris is born on June 15 in Albuquerque, New Mexico.

1975 David Michael Burtka is born on May 29 in Dearborn, Michigan.

1983 Harris is cast in his first play, as Toto in *The Wizard of Oz*.

1988 The movie *Clara's Heart* is released in theaters.

1989 Harris auditions for and wins the starring role in the TV show *Doogie Howser, M.D.*

1991 Harris graduates from La Cuyea High School.

1993 Burtka graduates from Plymouth Salem High School and begins college at the University of Michigan.

1997 Harris is cast as a member of the touring company of the Broadway musical *Rent*. Burtka graduates from the University of Michigan with a degree in Musical Theatre and moves to New York to become an actor. Burtka is cast in the musical *Children of Eden*.

2001 Burtka wins a Clarence Derwent Award for his work in the drama *The Play About the Baby*.

2003 Burtka is cast as Tulsa in *Gypsy*.

2004 Harris and Burtka meet for the first time and eventually start dating. Burtka first plays Matt in *The Opposite of Sex*.

2005 The sitcom *How I Met Your Mother* begins airing with Harris playing Barney Stinson.

2006 Harris comes out as gay in a statement to *People* magazine.

2009 Burtka begins studying to become a chef at Le Cordon Bleu. Harris hosts the Tony Awards for the first time.

2010 Harris and Burtka become fathers when their twins, Harper Grace and Gideon Scott, are born to a surrogate mother. Burtka starts a catering company with classmate Molly Hanissee.

2014 Harris and Burtka move their family back to New York. Burtka and Harris get married in Italy. Harris wins a Tony Award for his performance in *Hedwig and the Angry Inch*.

2015 Harris hosts the Academy Awards.

2017 *A Series of Unfortunate Events* begins airing on Netflix, with Harris as Count Olaf.

2018 The first episode of *Genius Junior* airs on NBC.

acclaim To praise something publicly and enthusiastically.

advocate A person who acts in support of something, such as a cause or another person.

ambition The desire to reach a particular goal.

audition A test that involves acting, singing, dancing, or playing an instrument to show one's skills.

burlesque hall A place where stage entertainment like singing, comedic skits, and songs are performed.

critic Someone who judges and examines the artistic merit of something, such as a movie, especially in a professional capacity.

disillusioned A lasting feeling of intense disappointment when something does not meet one's expectations.

heartthrob A person who is romantically desirable.

musical A play or movie that uses songs to help tell the story.

narrate To tell a story or describe the events taking place in a movie, book, or television show.

nomination The proposal of someone as a candidate for an award or office.

parody A project that loosely imitates another to make people laugh.

pilot An episode of a television show that is made to provide a sample of what a series will be like.

premiere The first public performance or showing, such as a musical work or movie.

prescription Instructions written by doctors to patients that tell how to take medicine.

producer A person who helps pay for or oversee a project such as a movie that will be shown to the public.

revival In theater, bringing an older play or musical back on stage, often with new actors or sets.

seminar A class designed for a small group of students in which ideas can be closely discussed.

sitcom A television show in which the characters handle different situations in a humorous way.

versatile Possessing a wide variety of different skills and abilities.

Academy of Canadian Cinema and Television
411 Richmond Street East, Suite 9
Toronto, ON M5A 3S5
Canada
Website: https://www.academy.ca
Facebook and Twitter: @TheCdnAcademy
Instagram: @thecdnacademy
The Academy of Canadian Cinema and Television
honors achievements in film, television, and
digital media.

Academy of Motion Picture Arts and Sciences
Academy Headquarters
8949 Wilshire Boulevard
Beverly Hills, CA 90211
(310) 247-3000
Website: https://www.oscars.org
Facebook: @Oscars.Academy
Instagram: @theacademy
Twitter: @TheAcademy
The Academy of Motion Picture Arts and Sciences
presents the Oscars awards every year. Its
members are actors, directors, and other film
industry professionals.

Academy of Television Arts and Sciences
Television Academy
5220 Lankershim Boulevard
North Hollywood, CA 91601
(818) 754-2800

Website: https://www.emmys.com
Facebook, Instagram, and Twitter:
    @televisionacad
As the organization that hands out the Emmy
    Awards each year, the Academy of Television
    Arts and Sciences honors recognizes excellence
    in daytime and primetime television.

American Theatre Wing
230 West 41st Street
New York, NY 10036
(212) 765-0606
Website: http://www.americantheatrewing.org
Facebook: @TheAmericanTheatreWing
Instagram: @thewing
Twitter: @TheWing
The American Theatre Wing promotes excellence
    and education in the theatrical arts. The
    organization honors outstanding productions
    with the annual Tony Awards.

Le Cordon Bleu
1460 Broadway
New York, NY 10036
(844) 280-1009
Website: https://www.cordonbleu.edu
Facebook: @lecordonbleuinternational
Instagram: @lecordonbleu_international
Twitter: @lecordonbleuint
As a renowned and global network of culinary

and hospitality schools, Le Cordon Bleu offers a range of degree programs for aspiring chefs, cooks, and restaurant managers.

Professional Association of Canadian Theatres
Artscape Distillery Studios
15 Case Goods Lane, Unit 201
Toronto, ON M5A 3C4
Canada
(800) 263-7228
Website: https://pact.ca
Facebook: @pactpage
Twitter: @PACTtweets
By advocating for the importance of live theater, the Professional Association of Canadian Theatres helps its members carry out their creative work within a supportive national network.

Bjorklund, Ruth. *Singing in Theater.* New York, NY: Cavendish Square, 2018.

Capaccio, George. *Acting in Theater.* New York, NY: Cavendish Square, 2017.

Capaccio, George. *How Rent Made It to the Stage.* New York, NY: Cavendish Square, 2018.

Cartlidge, Cherese. *Neil Patrick Harris.* San Diego, CA: Lucent Books, 2012.

Hurt, Avery Elizabeth. *Confronting LGBTQ+ Discrimination* (Speak Up! Confronting Discrimination in Your Daily Life). New York, NY: Rosen Publishing, 2018.

Kawa, Katie. *Television: The Small Box That Changed the World.* San Diego, CA: Lucent Books, 2018.

Machajewski, Sarah. *Cool Careers Without College for People Who Love to Cook & Eat.* Rosen Publishing, 2014.

McCarthy, Cecilia Pinto. *The Science of Movies.* Minneapolis, MN: Core Library, 2016.

Morlock, Theresa. *LGBTQ Human Rights Movement.* New York, NY: Rosen Publishing, 2017.

Paige, Elaine. *Musicals: The Definitive Illustrated Story.* New York, NY: DK, 2015.

Penne, Barbra. *Your Rights as an LGBTQ+ Teen* (The LGBTQ+ Guide to Beating Bullying). New York, NY: Rosen Publishing, 2018.

Zenon, Paul. *Street Tricks, Sleight of Hand and Illusion.* London, UK: Carlton Books, 2013.

Adams, Cindy. "David Burtka on Balancing Family and Broadway." *Page Six*, March 15, 2015. https://pagesix.com/2015/03/15/david-burtka -on-balancing-family-and-broadway.

Ainscough, Richard. "David Burtka: The Daily Grind." *Montecristo Magazine*, November 23, 2015. http://montecristomagazine.com /business/david-burtka.

Azzopardi, Chris. "From Commercial King to 'Kitchen Bitch.'" *Pride Source*, September 3, 2009. https://pridesource.com/article/37202.

Broadway.com. "The Opposite of Sex Extends San Fran Run." October 13, 2004. https://www .broadway.com/buzz/93779/the-opposite-of -sex-extends-san-fran-run.

BroadwayWorld. "David Burtka Biography." Retrieved October 23, 2018. https://www .broadwayworld.com/people/bio/David -Burtka.

Brown, Elizabeth Quinn. "Neil Patrick Harris Has a 'No Screens' Policy at His Family's Dinner Table." *Architectural Digest*, July 3, 2018. https://www.architecturaldigest.com/story/neil -patrick-harris-has-a-no-screens-policy-at-his -familys-dinner-table.

Business Wire. "'Project Last Mile' Expands to Liberia and Swaziland, Strengthening Health Systems across Africa." June 8, 2017. https:// www.businesswire.com/news /home/20170608005380/en.

Chuba, Kirsten. "Neil Patrick Harris Put His 'Heart' Into His First Film in 1987." *Variety*, March 23, 2018. https://variety.com/2018/vintage /features/actor-neil-patrick-harris-1202731627.

Daniels, Robert L. "Children of Eden." *Variety*, November 29, 1997. https://variety.com/1997 /legit/reviews/children-of-eden-111721434.

Dransfeldt, Jeffrey. "Harris Is Enjoying Barney's Adventures in 'How I Met Your Mother.'" *Ventura County Star*, April 26, 2008. https:// web.archive.org/web/20090314121342 /http://www.venturacountystar.com/news /2008/apr/26/well-dressed-womanizer.

Dulin, Dann. "David Burtka: Cover Story." *A&U*, April 5, 2014. https://aumag.org/2014/04 /05/david-burtka.

Dziemianowicz, Joe. "David Burtka, Neil Patrick Harris's Husband, Pulls Out of a Slump with Their Move to New York." *New York Daily News*, November 5, 2014. http://www .nydailynews.com/entertainment/back-nyc-neil -patrick-harris-david-burtka-blossoms-article -1.1999027.

Eisenberg, Eric. "Neil Patrick Harris Discusses the Escalation of NPH in *A Very Harold and Kumar 3D Christmas*." CinemaBlend, November 4, 2011. https://www.cinemablend.com/new/Neil -Patrick-Harris-Discusses-Escalation-NPH-Very -Harold-Kumar-3D-Christmas-27744.html.

Fecteau, Jessica. "David Burtka Is Releasing His First-Ever Cookbook." *People*, July 13, 2017.

https://people.com/food/david-burtka
-cookbook-lifes-a-party.

Goldberg, Lesley, and Kate Stanhope. "NBC
Greenlights 'Genius Junior' Game Show
Hosted by Neil Patrick Harris." *Hollywood
Reporter*, March 31, 2017. https://www
.hollywoodreporter.com/live-feed/nbc
-greenlights-genius-junior-game-show-hosted
-by-neil-patrick-harris-990454.

Grow, Kory. "Neil Patrick Harris Declined
Letterman's Job Because He'd 'Get Bored.'"
Rolling Stone, May 14, 2014. https://www
.rollingstone.com/tv/tv-news/neil-patrick
-harris-declined-lettermans-job-because-hed
-get-bored-90528.

Harris, Neil Patrick. *Neil Patrick Harris: Choose
Your Own Autobiography*. New York, NY:
Crown Archetype, 2014.

Harris, Neil Patrick, and David Burtka. "When
Stars Collide." *Out*, January 18, 2012. https://
www.out.com/out-exclusives/2012/01/11/neil
-patrick-harris-david-burtka-love-couple-stars
-children.

Hiatt, Brian. "How Neil Patrick Harris Met
Himself." *Rolling Stone*, May 22, 2014. https://
www.rollingstone.com/tv/tv-news/how-neil
-patrick-harris-met-himself-57783.

Huffington Post. "David Burtka Shares His New
York Favorites and His Plan for the Perfect Date
Night with Neil Patrick Harris." December 6,
2017. https://www.huffingtonpost

.com/2015/03/17/david-burtka-it-shoulda
-been-you-_n_6880832.html.

Internet Movie Database. "How I Met Your
Mother." Retrieved October 23, 2018. http://
imdb.com/title/tt0460649/?ref_=nv_sr_1.

Internet Movie Database. "Neil Patrick Harris."
Retrieved October 23, 2018. https://www
.imdb.com/name/nm0000439.

Kaufman, Joanne. "Neil Patrick Harris Finds a
Winning Rx in *Doogie Howser*." *People*, March
19, 1990. https://people.com/archive/neil
-patrick-harris-finds-a-winning-rx-in-doogie
-howser-vol-33-no-11.

LaFrance, Adrienne. "What Kind of Computer Did
Doogie Howser Have?" *The Atlantic*, October
13, 2015. https://www.theatlantic.com/notes
/2015/10/what-kind-of-computer-did-doogie
-howser-have/410266.

Leland, John. "O.K., You're Gay. So? Where's My
Grandchild?" *New York Times*, December 21,
2000. https://www.nytimes.com/2000/12/21
/garden/ok-you-re-gay-so-where-s-my
-grandchild.html.

Leonard, Elizabeth. "Neil Patrick Harris Marries
David Burtka." *People*, September 8, 2014.
https://people.com/celebrity/neil-patrick-harris
-marries-david-burtka.

Nahra, Ali. "Food & Family: An Interview With
Neil Patrick Harris and David Burtka." Spoon

University, September 5, 2018. https://
spoonuniversity.com/lifestyle/food-family-an
-interview-with-neil-patrick-harris-and-david
-burtka.

Nussbaum, Emily. "High-Wire Act." *New York*,
September 13, 2009. http://nymag.com/arts
/tv/profiles/59002/index3.html.

Ortegon, Josie. "Borderland's Ties to Oscars:
Neil Patrick Harris Discovered By Local Award-
Winning Playwright." KBIA-ABC 7, updated
August 24, 2016. https://www.kvia.com/news
/borderlands-ties-to-oscars-host-neil-patrick
-harris-discovered-by-local-award-winning
-playwright/56431955.

Otterson, Joe. "NBC Orders Neil Patrick Harris
Game Show 'Genius Junior.' *Variety*, March 31,
2017. https://variety.com/2017/tv/news/nbc
-neil-patrick-harris-genius-junior-1202020310.

OWN. "Neil Patrick Harris and David Burtka's
Families Speak Out." *Oprah's Next Chapter*.
Retrieved October 23, 2018. http://www
.oprah.com/own-oprahs-next-chapter/neil
-patrick-harris-and-david-burtkas-families
-speak-out-video.

Parker, Heidi. "They're Married! Neil Patrick
Harris Weds Partner of 10 Years David Burtka
During Intimate Ceremony in Italy." *Daily Mail*,
September 8, 2014. http://www.dailymail.co
.uk/tvshowbiz/article-2747929/Neil-Patrick

-Harris-weds-partner-10-years-David-Burtka
-intimate-ceremony-Italy.html.

Peanut Butter Players. "About Us."
Retrieved November 14, 2018. https://
peanutbutterplayers.com/about-us.

People. "Neil Patrick Harris Tells PEOPLE He Is
Gay." November 3, 2006. https://people.com
/celebrity/exclusive-neil-patrick-harris-tells
-people-he-is-gay.

Praderio, Caroline. "Neil Patrick Harris and His
Family Always Nail Halloween—Here are Their
Incredible Costumes." Insider, October 31,
2017. https://www.thisisinsider.com/neil
-patrick-harris-halloween-costumes-2016-10.

Robinson, Tasha. "Interview: Neil Patrick Harris."
A.V. Club, September 16, 2018. https://
tv.avclub.com/neil-patrick-harris-1798214813.

Rudetsky, Seth. "Onstage & Backstage: Going
Backwards in Time with David Burtka to His
Near-Death Experience in Peter Pan." *Playbill*,
December 1, 2014. http://www.playbill.com
/article/onstage-backstage-going-backwards
-in-time-with-david-burtka-to-his-near-death
-experience-in-peter-pan-com-336339.

Sanello, Frank. "Harris Just What Doctor Ordered
for 'Doogie.'" *Chicago Tribune*, August 19,
1990. http://www.chicagotribune.com/news
/ct-xpm-1990-08-19-9003100096-story.html.

Waldron, William. "See Neil Patrick Harris and
David Burtka's House in New York City."

Architectural Digest, December 30, 2016.
https://www.architecturaldigest.com/story/neil
-patrick-harris-david-burtka-harlem-townhouse
-article.

Willis, Haisten. "Neil Patrick Harris Speaks on
Reading at Major Conference for Librarians."
Atlanta Journal-Constitution, January 23, 2017.
https://www.ajc.com/lifestyles/neil-patrick
-harris-speaks-reading-major-conference-for
-librarians/XU1ahAIVTC6JOUnybxwzNK.

Yuan, Jada. "Neil Patrick Harris Interview:
'Coming Out? No One Seemed Bothered.'"
The Telegraph, February 22, 2015. https://
www.telegraph.co.uk/culture/film/film-news
/10828877/Neil-Patrick-Harris-interview
-Coming-out-No-one-seemed-bothered.html.

ABOUT THE AUTHOR

Jason Porterfield is a journalist and author living in Chicago, Illinois. He has written several biographies for young adults, including those on Calvin Hill and Grant Hill, Niklas Zennström, Tim Berners-Lee, Marco Polo, Voltaire, and Annie Oakley. Like Neil Patrick Harris, Porterfield was fascinated by magic while growing up and still remembers how to do a few card tricks.

PHOTO CREDITS

Design and Layout: Nicole Russo-Duca; Senior Editor: Kathy Kuhtz Campbell; Photo Researcher: Sherri Jackson